GREAT PRO SPORTS CHAMPIONSHIPS

GREAT NHL STANLEY CUP CHAMPIONSHIPS

by Ethan Olson

BrightPoint Press

San Diego, CA

© 2024 BrightPoint Press
an imprint of ReferencePoint Press, Inc.
Printed in the United States

For more information, contact:
BrightPoint Press
PO Box 27779
San Diego, CA 92198
www.BrightPointPress.com

ALL RIGHTS RESERVED.

No part of this work covered by the copyright hereon may be reproduced or used in any form or by any means—graphic, electronic, or mechanical, including photocopying, recording, taping, web distribution, or information storage retrieval systems—without the written permission of the publisher.

LIBRARY OF CONGRESS CATALOGING-IN-PUBLICATION DATA

Names: Olson, Ethan, author.
Title: Great NHL Stanley Cup championships / by Ethan Olson.
Description: San Diego, CA: BrightPoint, [2024] | Series: Great pro sports championships | Includes bibliographical references and index. | Audience: Ages 13 | Audience: Grades 7–9
Identifiers: LCCN 2023014648 (print) | LCCN 2023014649 (eBook) | ISBN 9781678206581 (hardcover) | ISBN 9781678206598 (eBook)
Subjects: LCSH: Stanley Cup (Hockey)--History--Juvenile literature. | National Hockey League--History--Juvenile literature. | Hockey--United States--History--Juvenile literature. | Hockey--Canada--History--Juvenile literature.
Classification: LCC GV847.7 .O66 2024 (print) | LCC GV847.7 (eBook) | DDC 796.962/648--dc23/eng/20230330
LC record available at https://lccn.loc.gov/2023014648
LC eBook record available at https://lccn.loc.gov/2023014649

CONTENTS

AT A GLANCE	4
INTRODUCTION QUEST FOR THE CUP	6
CHAPTER ONE SHAKING A DYNASTY	10
CHAPTER TWO REVERSING THE CURSE	22
CHAPTER THREE FOR RAY	34
CHAPTER FOUR PENGUIN PRIDE	46
Glossary	58
Source Notes	59
For Further Research	60
Index	62
Image Credits	63
About the Author	64

AT A GLANCE

- The Stanley Cup is awarded to the National Hockey League (NHL) champion. It was first given out in 1893. It is the oldest trophy in North American professional sports.

- The Edmonton Oilers were one of the NHL's most dominant teams in the 1980s. In 1987, Edmonton won its third Stanley Cup in four years. But the Oilers were pushed to the limit by the scrappy Philadelphia Flyers.

- The New York Rangers faced the Vancouver Canucks in the 1994 Stanley Cup Final. It had been fifty-four years since New York last lifted the trophy. The Rangers finally ended their drought in a dramatic series.

- In 2001, the Colorado Avalanche captured the Stanley Cup for the second time in six years. It was a special moment for Colorado defenseman

Ray Bourque. The superstar finally lifted the Cup for the first time in his twenty-second season.

- In 2009, the powerhouse Detroit Red Wings met the Pittsburgh Penguins for the second consecutive Stanley Cup Final. Pittsburgh's budding dynasty avenged a loss from the year before in a series that came down to the final shot.

INTRODUCTION

QUEST FOR THE CUP

Game 7 of the 2009 Stanley Cup Final was scoreless after one period. Early in the second period, Detroit Red Wings defenseman Brad Stuart controlled a loose puck behind his own net. He looked to pass ahead. His pass hit the skate of Pittsburgh's Evgeni Malkin. The puck bounced to

Maxime Talbot right in front of the Detroit net. Talbot needed only two touches to gather the puck. He slid a shot past Detroit goaltender Chris Osgood and gave the Penguins a 1–0 lead.

Pittsburgh Penguins center Maxime Talbot (25) beats Detroit Red Wings goalie Chris Osgood for a goal in Game 7 of the 2009 Stanley Cup Final.

It was the first of two goals for Talbot in the game. His play helped Pittsburgh upset the veteran Red Wings and take home Pittsburgh's first title in seventeen years.

HOCKEY'S TOP PRIZE

Performances like Talbot's add to the ever-growing lore of the Stanley Cup. The trophy is covered with the names of teams and players who have won it. Along the way, the chase for the top prize in the National Hockey League (NHL) has created many dramatic Stanley Cup Final series.

Talbot raises the Stanley Cup after the Penguins' win in 2009.

1
SHAKING A DYNASTY

The Edmonton Oilers and Philadelphia Flyers finished with the two best records in the 1986–87 NHL season. But not many people gave the Flyers a chance against the powerhouse Oilers in the 1987 Stanley Cup Final. Edmonton was looking for its third championship in four years.

Wayne Gretzky, the sport's all-time greatest scorer, led the way. He was just one of several stars for the Oilers. Others included center Mark Messier and winger Jari Kurri.

Wayne Gretzky led the NHL with 62 goals and 121 assists in 1986–87.

Edmonton had lost only two playoff games on its way to the 1987 Final.

Philadelphia had to battle its way through three tough series to reach the Final. Along the way, the Flyers lost leading scorer Tim Kerr to an injury. They looked overmatched in Game 1 as Edmonton won 4–2.

TWO COMEBACKS

The Flyers held a 2–1 lead after two periods of Game 2. But Edmonton's Glenn Anderson tied the game 11:40 into the third. In overtime, Gretzky streaked into the Flyers' zone before stopping along the

MOST STANLEY CUP VICTORIES OF ALL TIME

Montreal Canadiens . . . 23

Toronto Maple Leafs . . . 13

Detroit Red Wings 11

Boston Bruins 6

Chicago Blackhawks . . . 6

*Through the 2021–22 season

Source: "Playoff Team Records," National Hockey League, n.d. www.nhl.com.

The Montreal Canadiens have won the most all-time Stanley Cups.

right wall. He fired a pass across the ice to defenseman Paul Coffey. As the Flyers chased the puck, they left Kurri all alone in front of the net. Coffey slid a pass to Kurri, who buried the game-winning goal.

Down 2–0 in the series, the Flyers returned home to Philadelphia, Pennsylvania. There they hoped to get a boost from the rowdy fans at their home arena, the Spectrum. However, the Oilers raced out to a 3–0 lead early in the second period.

The Flyers weren't out of it, though. They scored twice before the period was over. Then Philadelphia winger Scott Mellanby tied the game on a **slap shot** at the 4:37 mark of the third. Just seventeen seconds later, Mellanby fed defenseman Brad McCrimmon with a cross-ice pass.

The Oilers finished the 1986–87 regular season with a record of 50–24–6.

McCrimmon beat Edmonton goalie Grant Fuhr to make it 4–3. It was the first time any team had ever come back from being down 3–0 to win a Stanley Cup Final game.

The Game 3 collapse didn't bother the Oilers. Edmonton dominated Game 4 and won 4–1. The Flyers were now down 3–1 in the series. Game 5 was back in Edmonton, Alberta. Edmonton jumped out to another early lead.

Philadelphia trailed 3–1 eight minutes into the second period. Flyers winger Brian

THE SLASH

In the third period of Game 4, frustrated Flyers goalie Ron Hextall slashed one of the Oilers in the back of the legs with his goal stick. Hextall was suspended for eight games. But he was able to finish the series. The punishment did not kick in until the start of the next season.

Propp then led another comeback. He had **assists** on three straight goals as Philadelphia won 4–3. Flyers goalie Ron Hextall also stopped 31 shots.

SHAKING THE SPECTRUM

The series returned to the Spectrum for Game 6. Once again, the Oilers took the lead. It was 2–1 Edmonton with eight minutes to play in the game. But Anderson took a high-sticking penalty. On Philadelphia's **power play**, Propp tied it up. The goal brought a roar from the crowd. It stayed noisy as the game restarted.

Less than two minutes later, the Flyers broke into the Edmonton zone. A loose puck popped out to an open space by the blue line. Philadelphia defenseman J.J. Daigneault stepped up and ripped a slap shot. It found its way through a crowd of players to beat Fuhr. The fans inside the packed arena exploded in celebration.

"I came off the ice and J.J. was my replacement: he came in and smoked it," said Flyers defenseman Mark Howe. "I remember sitting on the bench and thinking the roof was going to cave in because it was so loud."[1]

The Spectrum (front) was the Flyers' home arena from 1967 to 1996.

The Spectrum had opened in 1967. The noise after Daigneault's goal was thought to be the loudest moment in the arena's history. It became known as "The Night the Spectrum Shook."

The goal also won the game. The 3–2 score forced Game 7 in Edmonton. This time the Flyers jumped out to a lead on a power play goal just 1:41 into the first period.

From there the Oilers pelted Hextall with 43 shots. Messier tied the game before the end of the first. In the second, Gretzky spotted Kurri open at the left face-off dot. Kurri's wrist shot beat Hextall to make it 2–1.

The Flyers couldn't rally this time. They managed only two shots on Fuhr in the third period. Anderson sealed the win on a slap shot with 2:24 left in the game. The Flyers had made most of the big memories in the series. But in the end, the Oilers **dynasty** won out.

Gretzky holds up the Stanley Cup after the Oilers win in Game 7.

2
REVERSING THE CURSE

The New York Rangers are one of the oldest NHL teams. The team's history dates back to 1926. But most of that history seemed cursed for Rangers fans.

By the 1993–94 season, the New York Rangers had not won the Stanley Cup in fifty-four years. But in 1993–94, the team had the NHL's best record. The Rangers were led by captain Mark Messier. He had already won four championships with the Edmonton Oilers. After two easy playoff series, the Rangers beat the New Jersey Devils 4–3 to reach the Stanley Cup Final.

Mark Messier (right) battles for the puck with Vancouver's Trevor Linden during the 1994 Stanley Cup Final.

The surprising Vancouver Canucks were waiting. The Canucks were the seventh seed in the West. They upset three higher-seeded teams to reach the Final.

Many expected the Rangers to win the series easily. And New York came out firing in Game 1. The Rangers took 54 shots at Vancouver goaltender Kirk McLean's net.

A MESSIER GUARANTEE

The Rangers were down 3–2 to the New Jersey Devils entering Game 6 of the Eastern **Conference** finals. New York's Mark Messier told reporters that the Rangers would definitely win Game 6. He backed up his bold talk with three goals in a 4–2 win. The Rangers then won Game 7 in double overtime.

But McLean kept the score 1–1 until New York winger Alex Kovalev broke the tie 8:29 into the third period.

Vancouver winger Martin Gelinas scored from close range with one minute left to force overtime. With less than a minute left in the extra period, Rangers defenseman Brian Leetch hit the **crossbar** with a wrist shot. The Canucks gathered the puck and came down on a three-on-one break. Vancouver's Cliff Ronning passed to Greg Adams all alone in front of the net. Adams scored the winning goal. The Rangers had outshot Vancouver 54–31 but still lost.

Vancouver goalie Kirk McLean won 23 games during the 1993–94 regular season. He then won 15 in the playoffs.

RANGERS ROLL

For the next three games, the Rangers dominated. They won the second game 3–1. Game 3 moved the series to Vancouver, British Columbia. The Canucks were routed 5–1. Vancouver's star winger Pavel Bure was also thrown out of the game. He had high-sticked a New York player in the face during the first period.

The Canucks went up 2–1 in Game 4. Then New York goalie Mike Richter stuffed a **penalty shot** attempt from Bure. The Rangers then charged back. Leetch had a goal and three assists in a 4–2 victory. Game 5 was back in New York, New York. The Rangers had a chance to wrap it up at home.

The Canucks' Pavel Bure battles for position between New York defenseman Brian Leetch (left) and goalie Mike Richter (right).

AN ELECTRIC AFFAIR

Game 5 was 1–0 Vancouver when the third period began. Then the two teams started piling up goals. The Canucks scored twice in the first three minutes. The Rangers battled back with three goals in less than six minutes. The third, from Messier, tied the score.

The New York crowd's excitement didn't last long. Vancouver's Dave Babych put his team up 4–3 just twenty-nine seconds later. The Canucks added two more goals to send the series back to Vancouver.

The Canucks kept it going in Game 6. McLean made 28 saves in a 4–1 win. What looked like a comfortable series for the Rangers just four days earlier was now headed back to New York. And everything was on the line.

Messier celebrates after scoring in the second period of Game 7.

THE WAIT IS OVER

The rowdy crowd at Madison Square Garden got an early boost. Leetch and winger Adam Graves scored less than four minutes apart to make it 2–0. An early second-period goal from Vancouver captain Trevor Linden tightened things up. With 7:31 left the Rangers were on a power play. Messier poked home a rebound to make the score 3–1.

Linden scored again less than five minutes into the third period. Fans roared for the rest of the game, urging the Rangers to hold the lead. The Canucks hit the post twice but could not beat Richter.

The final thirty-seven seconds saw three tense face-offs in the New York end.

The last came with 1.6 seconds left. The referees had to stop play to make sure they had the correct time. During the wait, the crowd chanted loudly. As the clock finally hit zero, Madison Square Garden exploded in celebration. So did New York's radio announcers, Sam Rosen and John Davidson.

"The waiting is over. The New York Rangers are Stanley Cup champions! And this one will last a lifetime!" Rosen exclaimed.

"No more curses!" Davidson added.[2]

Richter hoists the Stanley Cup after the Rangers' victory.

3

FOR RAY

The Boston Bruins drafted defenseman Ray Bourque in 1979. Over the next twenty seasons, he became one of the most reliable players in the league. Bourque won many awards. He also won the respect of teammates, fans, and opponents for his great play.

Entering the 1999–2000 season, the one thing Bourque had not won was the Stanley Cup. His Bruins had been to the Final twice.

Ray Bourque played 1,518 NHL games in Boston before he was traded to the Colorado Avalanche in 2000.

They lost both. That year Boston was struggling. Bourque was thirty-nine years old. No one had played more NHL games than Bourque without winning a Stanley Cup. He asked general manager Harry Sinden for a trade. He wanted to go to a team with a chance to win it all. Sinden traded Bourque to the Colorado Avalanche.

The plan didn't work. The Avalanche lost to the Dallas Stars in the Western Conference finals. The New Jersey Devils then beat Dallas to win the Stanley Cup.

Bourque returned to Colorado in 2000–01 for one more try. He had some

New Jersey goalie Martin Brodeur led the Devils to Stanley Cup wins in 1995, 2000, and 2003.

superstar teammates, such as goalie Patrick Roy, center Peter Forsberg, and center Joe Sakic, the team captain. All three had helped Colorado win the Cup in 1997.

Many people thought the Avalanche could win again in 2001.

Bourque had seven goals and fifty-two assists during the season, and Colorado made it back to the Stanley Cup Final. Waiting there were the Devils. They had won two Stanley Cups since 1995. Seemingly no one outside New Jersey was rooting against Bourque and the Avalanche.

Colorado rode that fan support to a 5–0 blowout Game 1 home win. Sakic led the way with two goals. Game 2 was closer. The Devils scored two late goals in the first period. They held on for a 2–1 win.

Petr Sykora (front) had two goals and two assists for the Devils during the 2001 Stanley Cup Final.

GAME WINNER

The series shifted to East Rutherford, New Jersey, for Game 3. It was tied 1–1 in the opening minute of the third period.

Sakic won a face-off in the New Jersey end. The puck went back to Bourque. The forty-year-old had space to move to the middle of the ice. He then ripped a slap shot past New Jersey's star goaltender Martin Brodeur.

Bourque's goal was the game winner. Colorado won 3–1. But the Devils bounced back again in Game 4. Colorado had a 2–1 lead early in the third period. Then New Jersey center Scott Gomez scored to make it 2–2. Devils winger Petr Sykora broke the tie with 2:37 left. New Jersey's 3–2 win sent the teams back to Denver, Colorado, even.

Joe Sakic played with the Avalanche franchise for 20 seasons. He is the team's all-time leader in goals scored and points.

The Devils ripped Colorado 4–1 in Game 5. Suddenly, it looked like Bourque might come up short of his dream again. Colorado had lost two straight. Now they had to win in New Jersey.

Roy, one of the best goaltenders ever, came to the rescue. He stopped 24 shots. Colorado skated away with a 4–0 win in Game 6. Now the series shifted back to Denver. All eyes returned to Bourque.

FINALLY

The Avalanche were trying to win the Stanley Cup for their oldest player. But it was one of the youngest members of the team who stepped up early in Game 7. Alex Tanguay was a twenty-one-year-old winger. He had scored 27 goals during the season. Just under eight minutes into the first period, Tanguay picked up a loose puck in the corner. He skated around the net and fired a high shot past Brodeur.

Tanguay scored again in the second period. Less than two minutes later, Sakic made it 3–0. The Devils scored late in the second. Throughout the third period,

BACK TO BOSTON

Fans in Boston, Massachusetts, never stopped loving Bourque. He paid them back during his ceremonial day with the Stanley Cup. Bourque took the trophy back to Boston. Thousands of fans came out to cheer for him at a rally in Boston's City Hall Plaza.

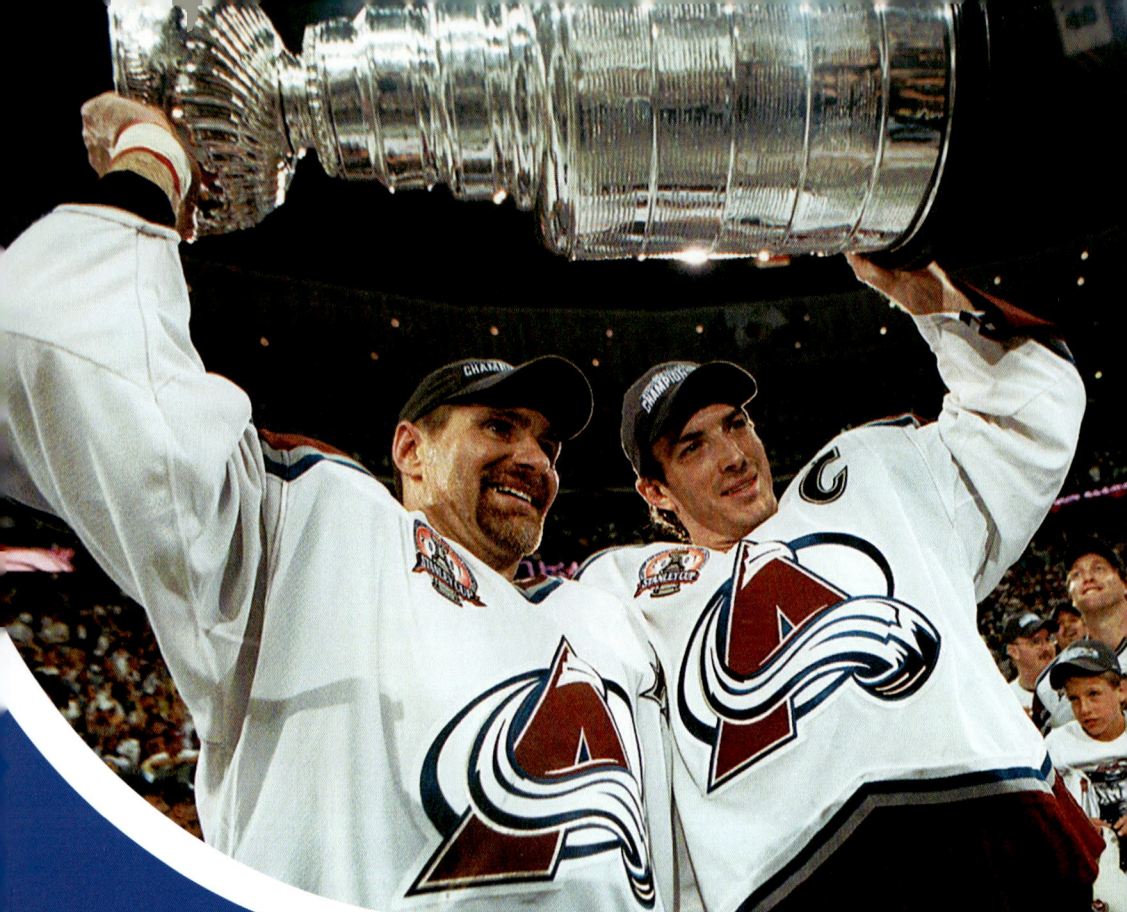

Bourque (left) and Sakic hold up the Stanley Cup after the Avalanche's victory in Game 7.

television cameras zoomed in on Bourque any time play stopped.

Bourque was nearly in tears late in the game. But his teammates urged him on. "I had a hard time breathing. I tried to get off.

The guys would push me back on the ice," Bourque said. "They wanted me out there for the final buzzer."[3]

One of the traditions of the Stanley Cup is for the captain to touch the trophy first. This time, Sakic barely had his hands on it before he handed it to Bourque. The crowd in Denver erupted as Bourque skated around with the trophy. One of the game's most respected players finally had the sport's ultimate prize.

"A name was missing from that [Cup]," said Roy after the game. "And today it is back to normal."[4]

4
PENGUIN PRIDE

In 2008, the Detroit Red Wings beat the Pittsburgh Penguins 4–2 to capture the Stanley Cup. It was Detroit's fourth victory in eleven years.

The Red Wings had veteran superstars like defenseman Nicklas Lidström and forwards Henrik Zetterberg and Pavel Datsyuk. Detroit fans expected more titles.

The Penguins also had a trio of great young players. Goalie Marc-André Fleury and center Evgeni Malkin were rising stars.

The Detroit Red Wings met the Pittsburgh Penguins in a Stanley Cup Final rematch in 2009. That had not happened in the NHL since 1984.

Center Sidney Crosby was considered the best young talent in the league.

Detroit and Pittsburgh met again in the Final the next year. As they got ready for the 2009 series, fans wondered if Pittsburgh could top Detroit's veterans. The Red Wings offered an answer in the first two games. Both were 3–1 Detroit wins. Goaltender Chris Osgood stopped 31 saves in each.

PENGUINS POUNCE

Back home in Pittsburgh, Pennsylvania, for Game 3, the Penguins finally got going. Malkin had three assists. Center Maxime

Red Wings goalie Chris Osgood had a 2.01 goals-against average in the 2009 playoffs.

Talbot scored twice. His second was an **empty net goal** with fifty-seven seconds left. That sealed the Penguins' 4–2 win.

Though Crosby was just twenty-one years old, he was already Pittsburgh's captain. Fans looked to him to lead the team. Yet through three games, "Sid the Kid" had just one assist. He came to life in Game 4. The game was tied 2–2 midway through the second period. Malkin fed Crosby to give Pittsburgh the lead. Crosby then assisted on Tyler Kennedy's goal in the third to secure another 4–2 Pittsburgh win.

The series was tied moving back to Detroit, Michigan. But one of the Red Wings' stars was ready to return to the action. Datsyuk had been injured in the

Western Conference finals. Now he was ready to play again.

Datsyuk's two assists were one boost for Detroit. Pittsburgh's penalty trouble was another. The Penguins took five minor penalties in the second period. Detroit scored on three power plays. It was enough to blow open a 5–0 Red Wings win.

RUSSIAN PRIDE

Pittsburgh's Evgeni Malkin won the Conn Smythe Trophy as the Most Valuable Player in the 2009 playoffs. He became the first Russian-born player to win the award. The twenty-two-year-old led the league with 36 playoff points.

JUST HOLD ON

Fleury hadn't always played well in the first five games. But he bounced back in Game 6, stopping 25 of 26 shots. The Penguins took a 2–1 lead into the final minute.

As Detroit scrambled for the tying goal, Fleury was forced to make an acrobatic save. He stopped the shot but slid out of the net. The puck dropped in front of the goal. Penguins defenseman Rob Scuderi knelt down to block the open goal mouth. He stuffed three attempts from Detroit's Johan Franzen before Fleury was able to cover the puck.

The referee signals no goal as players pile up in the crease following Rob Scuderi's blocked shots late in Game 6.

THE SAVE

Scuderi's heroics saved the win and forced Game 7 in Detroit. The two teams began the game slowly. But Detroit's Brad Stuart turned the puck over to Talbot 1:13 into the second period. Talbot's seventh playoff goal put Pittsburgh up 1–0.

A few minutes later, Crosby hobbled to the bench after being hit. He was quickly taken to the locker room. Though he returned for one shift in the third period, Crosby was mostly out of the game.

"You get to a point where you've got to ask yourself whether you're going to be hurting your team by being out there," Crosby said later.[5]

Without their captain, other Penguins had to step up. Talbot was ready. With just over

Sidney Crosby limps off the ice after being hit by Detroit's Johan Franzen in Game 7.

ten minutes left in the second, he scored again for a 2–0 lead.

Fleury made several big saves late in the second and early in the third.

Finally, Detroit's Jonathan Ericsson blasted a slap shot past Fleury with 6:07 left.

The Red Wings pulled Osgood for an extra skater in the final minute. With six seconds left, the teams had a face-off to Fleury's left. The puck popped out to Detroit defenseman Brian Rafalski at the blue line. He let go a slap shot that bounced off the crowd of players in front of the net.

The puck popped loose on the other side of the ice. Lidström scrambled after it. Fleury spotted the puck just in time to slide over. Lidström let go a shot that hit a diving Fleury right in the chest as time expired.

The Penguins celebrate with the Stanley Cup after winning their first championship in seventeen years.

The thrilling final seconds gave Pittsburgh its first Stanley Cup championship since 1992. Crosby had enough strength to hoist the Stanley Cup. He was the youngest captain to ever lift the trophy.

GLOSSARY

assists

passes or shots that lead to goals for teammates

conference

a grouping of teams that play in the NHL

crossbar

a horizontal post that connects the two vertical goalposts and forms the top edge of a goal

dynasty

a team that has an extended period of success

empty net goal

a goal scored after a team has removed its goalie to add an additional skater

penalty shot

a free shot given to a player who draws a penalty while on a breakaway

power play

the result of a penalty where the penalized team must play without five skaters on the ice for a period of time

slap shot

a hard shot made by raising the stick about waist high before hitting the puck

SOURCE NOTES

CHAPTER ONE: SHAKING A DYNASTY

1. Quoted in Mike Morreale, "J.J. Daigneault Goal in Game 6 of Stanley Cup Final Shook Spectrum: Capped Flyers' Comeback from Down Two Against Oilers," *National Hockey League*, May 28, 2017. www.nhl.com.

CHAPTER TWO: REVERSING THE CURSE

2. Quoted in "Rangers Win Stanley Cup | 6/14/1994," *YouTube*, uploaded by Ryan G, July 18, 2011. www.youtube.com.

CHAPTER THREE: FOR RAY

3. Quoted in "Ray Bourque Capped Career with Dramatic Cup in 2001," *YouTube*, uploaded by NHL, March 22, 2017. www.youtube.com.

4. Quoted in Jack Falla (editor), *Quest for the Cup: A History of the Stanley Cup Finals 1893–2001*. Toronto, ON: Key Porter Books, 2001, p. 266.

CHAPTER FOUR: PENGUIN PRIDE

5. Quoted in "Penguins Captain Sidney Crosby Injured in Game 7, Still Lifts the Stanley Cup," *NHL*, June 12, 2009. www.nhl.com.

FOR FURTHER RESEARCH

BOOKS

B. Keith Davidson, *NHL*. New York: Crabtree Publishing, 2021.

Anthony K. Hewson, *GOATs of Hockey*. Minneapolis, MN: Abdo Publishing, 2022.

Thom Storden, *Hockey's Greatest Game-Winning Goals and Other Crunch-Time Heroics*. Mankato, MN: Capstone Press, 2020

INTERNET SOURCES

Michael Farber, "Hoo-Ray! After a 22-Year Quest for an NHL Championship, Colorado's Ray Bourque Finally Laid Claim to the Cup," *Sports Illustrated*, June 18, 2001. www.vault.si.com.

Sean Leahy, "NBCSN's Stanley Cup Final Week: Remembering 2009 Penguins-Red Wings," *NBC Sports*, June 8, 2020. www.nhl.nbcsports.com.

Leigh Montville, "The Cup of Sorrow," *Sports Illustrated*, June 21, 1994. www.vault.si.com.

Mike Morreale, "J.J. Daigneault Goal in Game 6 of Stanley Cup Final Shook Spectrum: Capped Flyers' Comeback From Down Two Against Oilers," *National Hockey League*, May 28, 2017. www.nhl.com.

WEBSITES

Hockey Hall of Fame
www.hhof.com

The Hockey Hall of Fame is located in Toronto, Ontario, Canada. The hall's website has information on museum exhibits and artifacts, including the Stanley Cup.

Hockey Reference
www.hockey-reference.com

Hockey Reference is a research website that offers accurate statistical data for every game and player ever associated with the National Hockey League.

National Hockey League
www.nhl.com

NHL.com is the official website of the National Hockey League and all thirty-two of its member franchises.

INDEX

Adams, Greg, 25
Anderson, Glenn, 12, 17, 20

Babych, Dave, 29
Bourque, Ray, 34–36, 38, 40–42, 43, 44–45
Brodeur, Martin, 40, 43
Bure, Pavel, 27

Coffey, Paul, 13
Crosby, Sidney, 48, 50, 54, 57

Daigneault, J.J., 18–19
Datsyuk, Pavel, 47, 50–51
Davidson, John, 32

Ericsson, Jonathan, 56

Fleury, Marc-André, 47, 52, 55–56
Forsberg, Peter, 37
Franzen, Johan, 52
Fuhr, Grant, 15, 18, 20

Gelinas, Martin, 25
Gomez, Scott, 40
Graves, Adam, 31
Gretzky, Wayne, 11–12, 20

Hextall, Ron, 16, 17, 20
Howe, Mark, 18

Kennedy, Tyler, 50
Kerr, Tim, 12
Kovalev, Alex, 25
Kurri, Jari, 11, 13, 20

Leetch, Brian, 25, 27, 30
Lidström, Nicklas, 46, 56
Linden, Trevor, 31

Malkin, Evgeni, 6, 47–48, 50, 51
McCrimmon, Brad, 14–15
McLean, Kirk, 24–25, 29
Mellanby, Scott, 14
Messier, Mark, 11, 20, 23, 24, 29, 31

Osgood, Chris, 7, 48, 56

Propp, Brian, 17

Rafalski, Brian, 56
Richter, Mike, 27, 31
Ronning, Cliff, 25
Rosen, Sam, 32
Roy, Patrick, 37, 42, 45

Sakic, Joe, 37–38, 40, 43, 45
Scuderi, Rob, 52–53
Sinden, Harry, 36
Stuart, Brad, 6, 53
Sykora, Petr, 40

Talbot, Maxime, 6–8, 48–49, 54
Tanguay, Alex, 42–43

Zetterberg, Henrik, 47

IMAGE CREDITS

Cover: © Frank Gunn/The Canadian Press/AP Images
5: © Adwo/Shutterstock Images
7: © Frank Gunn/The Canadian Press/AP Images
9: © Paul Sancya/AP Images
11: © AP Images
13: © Red Line Editorial
15: © Rusty Kennedy/AP Images
19: © Tim Shaffer/AP Images
21: © Larry Macdougal/AP Images
23: © Bruce Bennett/Getty Images
26: © Graig Abel/Getty Images Sport/Getty Images
28: © Ron Frehm/AP Images
30: © Ron Frehm/AP Images
33: © Ron Frehm/AP Images
35: © IHA/Icon Sportswire
37: © Paul Chiasson/AP Images
39: © Daniel Hulshizer/AP Images
41: © IHA/Icon SMI 524/Newscom
44: © Bruce Bennett/Getty Images
47: © Keith Srakocic/AP Images
49: © Frank Gunn/The Canadian Press/AP Images
53: © Keith Srakocic/AP Images
55: © Paul Sancya/AP Images
57: © Paul Sancya/AP Images

ABOUT THE AUTHOR

Ethan Olson is a sportswriter and editor based in Minneapolis, Minnesota.